PICTURES · FROM · THE · PAST

The People's War

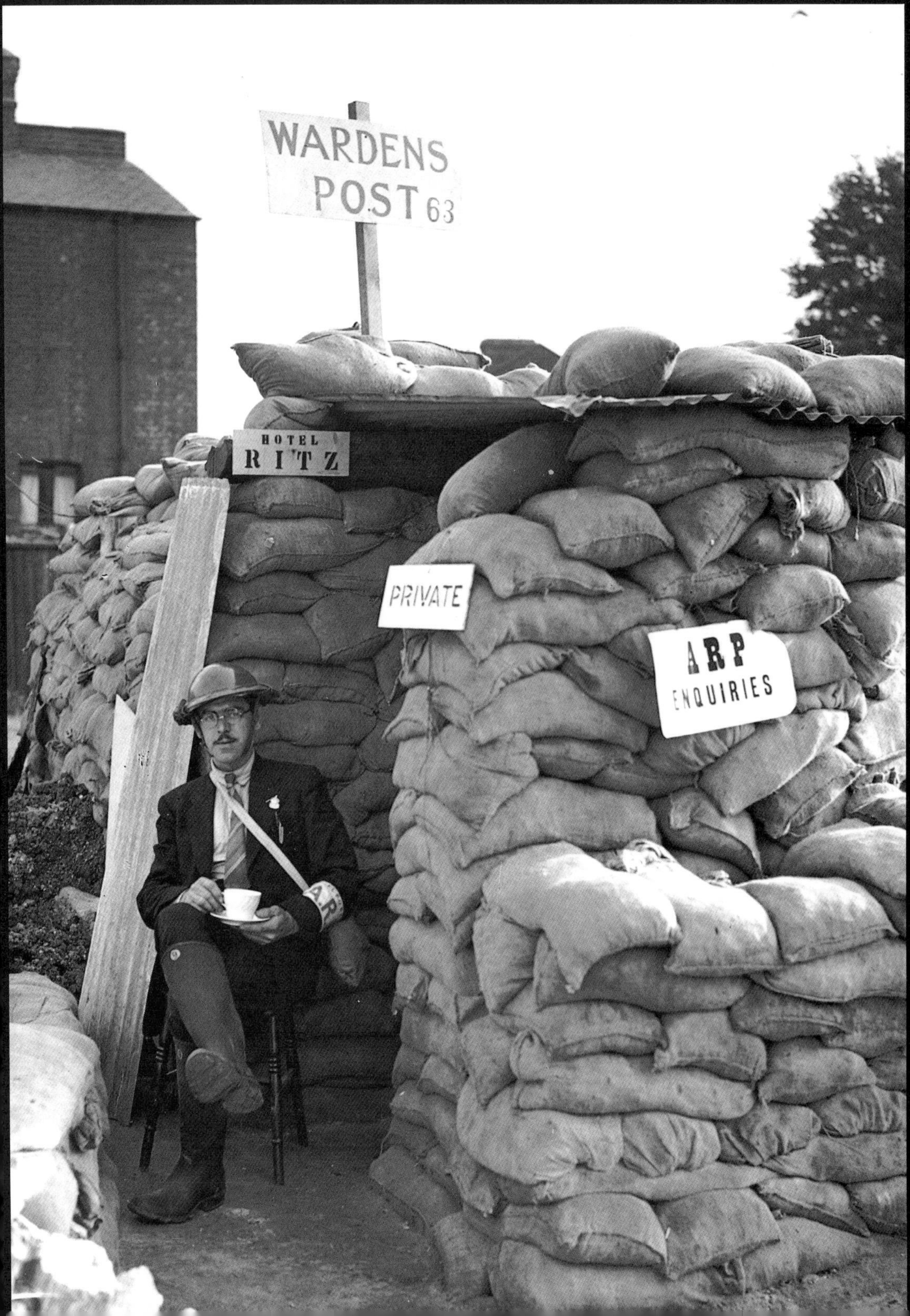

WARDENS POST 63
HOTEL RITZ
PRIVATE
ARP ENQUIRIES

PICTURES · FROM · THE · PAST

The People's War

Juliet Gardiner

SELECT
EDITIONS

First published in Great Britain in 1991
by Collins & Brown Limited

ISBN 1 85648 132 8

The pictures in this book are archive photographs and, to preserve the character and
quality of the original, have not been re-touched in any way.

Acknowledgements
The author and publishers are grateful to the Imperial War Museum for permission to
reproduce the following copyright photographs:
Pages 28 (both), 34 (bottom), 37, 49.

All other photographs were supplied by the Hulton Picture Company and are available as
framed prints. For more information and to place your orders contact:

Framed Prints
Hulton Picture Company
Unique House
21–31 Woodfield Road
London W9 2BA

Tel: 071 266 2660
Fax: 071 266 2414

This edition published 1993 by
The Promotional Reprint Co Ltd,
exclusively for Selecta Book Ltd,
Folly Road,Roundway, Devizes,
Wiltshire, SN10 2HR

Reprinted 1995(twice)

Printed in Hong Kong

Contents

INTRODUCTION

3 September 1939

'For a week now, everybody in London had been saying every day that if there wasn't a war tomorrow, there wouldn't be a war. Yesterday, people were saying that if there wasn't a war today, it would be a bloody shame. Now that there is a war, the English, slow to start, have in spirit, started and are comfortably two laps ahead of the official war machine, which had to await the drop of the handkerchief. In the general opinion, Hitler has it coming to him', wrote the *New Yorker*'s London correspondent as war broke out in Europe for the second time in just over twenty years.

But this time it was different. It wasn't only a soldier's war: it was a people's war too. Every-one's life changed dramatically, from the youngest to the oldest: not just those who marched away to war, but also the people left at home coping the best they could with the shortages, the inconveniences – and, in no small measure, the fear.

As Winston Churchill told the world in the summer of 1940: 'This is a war of unknown warriors. The whole of the warring nations are involved, not only soldiers but the entire population, men, women and children. The fronts are everywhere. The trenches are dug in towns and in the streets. Every village is fortified. Every road is barred. The front lines run through the factories. The workmen are soldiers with different weapons but the same courage.'

That courage and those weapons were part of the armoury of ordinary people's participation in the war. Hitler's aim was to blockade and bomb the civilian population into submission: had this happened the war would have

RIGHT: *The British ultimatum to Germany to withdraw its troops from Poland ran out at 11 o'clock on 3 September, 1939. Crowds watched silently as Big Ben struck the hour.*

been lost despite the most valiant efforts of the military. Digging allotments, pinning up blackout, 'saving and mending', tearing up your iron railings and gates for battleships and giving your saucepans and tin baths for aircraft production, billeting troops and taking in evacuees, queueing for hours and then mounting a wearisome campaign to feed a family on almost nothing recognisable and keep them warm with more dust than coal, clothe them when you were short of coupons and when there was hardly anything in the shops anyway: this was fighting for victory at home in the same war that the troops were fighting overseas.

It was the same war that demanded that men who were too old to fight or who were doing essential jobs that meant they couldn't be spared for the forces, were nevertheless required to turn out for fire-watching or blackout patrol, women who had never worked outside the home 'emerged from the herbaceous borders to answer the call of duty', whilst mothers who had thought that they worked round the clock before the war, nevertheless managed to 'fit in' a full-time job in war production.

From the start it was a war of instruction and exhortation: 'Careless Talk Costs Lives', 'Be Like Dad, Keep Mum', 'Is Your Journey Really Necessary?', 'Dig for Victory', 'Don't be a Squanderbug'. But these weren't just years of obedience and endurance. It took spirit and determination to enlist in the people's war. The home front would fight – but it would fight back too. The government might press for evacuation, but many parents brought their children home after a few months; regulations might forbid sleeping in the underground: people bought a $1\frac{1}{2}$d ticket and took a pillow down there anyway; if there were going to be shortages, there was the feeling that there should be rationing for everyone and fair shares for all.

The people's war meant bravery and sticking it out and coping and making do, and getting fed up and fighting on anyway. It was about being in the front line a lot of the time and getting battle-hardened so that you became determined that if you had to fight a people's war, then there ought to be a people's victory at the end of it.

BELOW: *Minutes after the Prime Minister, Neville Chamberlain, had declared war, the siren sounded. It was a false alarm. But it was war.*

BE PREPARED

The impact of war abroad was felt at home at once. A galaxy of silent, silver barrage balloons hovered in the sky, the blackout enveloped homes and made city streets and country roads hazardous and confusing.

Children were sent to the country, their parents willing; civil servants were despatched to spa towns and seaside resorts; the Bank of England removed itself to a small Hampshire town; sections of the BBC relocated to Worcester; and the 'Old Masters' from the National Gallery were transported to a deep quarry in Wales for the duration of the war. Livestock was evacuated; and whilst a few privileged pets were boarded out in the country in accommodation with 'a gas-proof dug-out and every care for 15 shillings a week', many more ended up in a heap outside the vet's – early victims of the threat of shortages and rationing: the uncertainties of war.

RIGHT: *Men prepare for the Second World War in the shadow of a memorial to the dead of the First. Scooping soil to fill sandbags at Hyde*

RIGHT: *Accidents increased in the blackout as city dwellers walked off pavements, knocked into lampposts or stepped into the path of cars with their headlights blotted out. Pedestrians were advised to wear a white carnation, carry a white pekinese – or leave their shirt tails hanging out.*

ABOVE: *'If the gas rattles sound, put your gas mask on at once, even in bed', instructed government leaflets. At first people obeyed, carrying their cardboard containers everywhere. In 1938, 38 million masks had been distributed, but by the spring of 1940 almost no one bothered anymore: the dangers of this war were to come in different guises.*

Official calculations anticipated 100,000 tons of bombs would fall on London in the first fourteen days. It was also assumed that the Germans would use poison gas, so gas masks were issued.

LEFT AND RIGHT: *The Grenadier Guards marched in gas masks through the Tower of London in pre-war practice, and neighbours 'talked' over the garden fence. Instructions were to put your chin in the mask first and spit on the mica window to stop it steaming up. The masks smelt of rubber and disinfectant and emitted odd, and not entirely polite, noises when you tried to speak.*

LEFT: *Chelsea Pensioners, veterans from an earlier war, gird themselves to meet the probable horrors of another round of conflict.*

The blackout united the population in immediate irritation with the war.

BELOW: *Precious time and money had to be spent in ensuring that there were heavy blackout curtains to draw every evening, or thick cardboard to be pinned to window frames – back and front – so that not a chink of light could escape.*

LEFT: *Some had problems of a different scale from others. The butler helps put up the blackout at Easton Neston in Northamptonshire.*

'*A blackout warden passin' by yelled,*
"*Ma, pull down that blind.*
Just look what you're showin''",
and we shouted, "Never mind".
Ooh! Knees up, Mother Brown.
Well, knees up, Mother Brown.'

RIGHT AND BELOW: *To help traffic – and pedestrians – white stripes were painted down the centre of roads, on kerbs, steps and lampposts. Torches were only allowed if they were permanently pointed at the ground and covered with two layers of tissue paper, and, in the early days of the war, cigarette smokers who lit up in the streets risked a zealous ARP warden yelling, 'Put it out!'*

To Churchill the time between September 1939 and April 1940 was a period of 'pretended war' – though the war at sea was real enough. But at one level London was prepared.

ABOVE: *The statue of Eros, the god of love, was removed from Piccadilly Circus. The neon lights no longer flashed in the Circus either, which some found a great improvement.*

LEFT: *A soldier in ceremonial dress on duty outside Marlborough House, equipped with a protective shelter adjacent to his sentry box.*

RIGHT: *Whitehall: Sandbags protected the doorways of important buildings, swaddled the concrete constructions used by ARP wardens and narrowed city streets to virtual towpaths in some places.*

'Since the war began, the Government has received countless inquiries from men of all ages who wish to do something for the defence of their country. Well now is your opportunity...', broadcast the Secretary for War, as the German tanks rolled into France. By the end of June, one and a half million men had volunteered for this citizen's army. They became part of a volunteer force which was prepared to defend Britain part-time, without pay, but with a uniform and equipment – of sorts.

LEFT: Women and those too old for active service were the backbone of the ARP. At first often regarded with exasperation – 'there are no plums in our job, only raspberries,' an ARP warden complained – many became heroes when the blitz started.

RIGHT: The 'vanishing Home Guard', an exercise in camouflage. The costume of torn sacks made the man 'indistinguishable from the bushes'.

BELOW: Guerrillas on parade. The Slough Women's Fighting Service go for their rifles during a training exercise in November 1941.

At the beginning of the war motorists were allowed the 'basic petrol ration', which was enough for about 120 miles of motoring a month. It was withdrawn altogether in 1942 and the two million cars on the road before the war fell to 700,000. Coupons were available for 'essential travel' and there was a brisk trade in black market coupons. Motorists could be stopped and asked 'Is your journey really necessary?' and were prosecuted and jailed for using 'essential' petrol for joy-riding.

BELOW: *Alternative methods of propulsion were experimented with. Horse-drawn transport was used for deliveries and shopping, as here in Cheltenham. The price of horses and ponies shot up at auction.*

LEFT: *The gas companies promoted a tank which sat on the roof of a vehicle and contained the equivalent of about a gallon of petrol. By May 1940 London had a network of supply points, but the idea never really caught on.*

Taking Shelter

'Almost no shelter is proof against a direct hit from a heavy bomb', warned a Ministry of Home Security pamphlet on sale for 3d in 1940, 'but the chances of your own home getting a direct hit are very small indeed'.

'Going to the shelter' was to become the nightly ritual for Londoners after the spring of 1940. The shelter might be a surface one, or perhaps a strengthened and sandbagged railway arch, or a trench dug in a park, or the underground. It could even be a 'natural shelter' (people took refuge in caves in the cliffs of Dover) – anywhere where they felt that they were safest from the threat of bombs.

RIGHT AND BELOW: *The most popular type of domestic shelter was the Anderson shelter, named after the Home Secretary. Distribution was started before the war broke out and provided free to those earning less than £250 a year; by September 1940 nearly a quarter of the population had one. It consisted of curved steel which was bolted together and had to be dug into the earth and covered with three feet of earth. The shelters were small, rather more suitable for storing bikes in, and they were liable to flood; but the main drawback was that many people in cities had no garden.*

THE BLITZ

'I see the damage done by the enemy ... but I also see the spirit of an unconquerable people.'

Winston Churchill

Almost a year after everyone had been expecting it, the *Blitzkrieg* came – and it was to last nearly a year. Bombs dropped almost nightly on London – and sometimes in the day too – until May 1941; and there were devastating and repeated raids on other industrial cities and ports – Liverpool, Plymouth, Manchester, Bristol, Cardiff, Birmingham, Hull, Coventry, Southampton ... The blitz put the cities of Britain in the front line of the war. When, in September 1940, an American expressed concern over civilians' morale in London, he was told firmly, 'There are no civilians in London'.

The fires that followed the bombs transformed Britain's cityscapes and the daily lives of the city dwellers, 'as the *Blitzkrieg* continues to be directed against such military objectives as the tired shop girl, the red-eyed clerk and the thousands of dazed and weary families patiently trudging their few belongings in perambulators away from the wreckage of their homes', in the words of Mollie Panter-Downs, London Correspondent of the *New Yorker*.

RIGHT: *On Saturday 7 September 1940, the Luftwaffe broke through the defences of Fighter Command and set London alight. Firewatchers stood on the colonnades of St Paul's Cathedral watching the docks and the city burn all around them. 'It's like the end of the world', one said. 'It is the end of a world', another replied. On 8 December another conflagration came very near to destroying Wren's city masterpiece, but when the All Clear sounded the Cathedral still stood in a wasteland of destruction.*

'Send all the bloody pumps you've got; the whole bloody world's on fire', signalled the Chief Fire Officer at Surrey Docks on 'Black Saturday'. Over 635 tonnes of high explosives and at least 800 bomb canisters fell on the capital. The raids took the lives of more than 400 Londoners and injured a further 16,000. They started fires which burned out of control all night – and some were still smouldering a week later. A pall of smoke two miles high rose into the sky which was as red and vivid as daylight.

ABOVE: *A hospital in south-east London was hit, but all the patients survived unharmed.*

LEFT: *A survivor of a raid stumbles from his bombed-out home, numb and covered in debris and dust.*

ABOVE: *May 1941. After eight and a half months of almost continual bombing raids, J.B. Priestley broadcast, 'We are not civilians who have happened to stray into a kind of hell on earth, but soldiers who have been flung into battle, perhaps the most important this war will see'. Up until September 1942, more civilians than servicemen had been killed and injured.*

ABOVE: *Going for cover. Communal brick shelters were never very popular – though the Ministry of Home Security tried its best with leaflets that urged 'you and your neighbours can spend many hours in comfort; you can … paper the walls … and whitewash the ceiling. A home-made heater can be made with two large flower pots'. But the public remained sceptical and preferred to go underground.*

LEFT: *Anywhere underground – cellars, coal holes, ditches, improvised trenches or, in this case, the crypt of Christ Church, Spitalfields – was deemed safer from attack by those without their own shelters at home – the vast majority of East Enders.*

ABOVE: *Rather than risk travelling during a raid after a night out, patrons of West End restaurants and night clubs would sometimes bed down on the floor after dinner, as in this photograph taken in the Hungaria restaurant in Soho.*

The War Goes Underground

By September 1940, 177,000 Londoners were using the underground as a shelter every night. The authorities had been opposed to the idea in case people developed a siege mentality and refused to come up again. Londoners took the matter into their own hands by buying a ticket and not travelling anywhere. There was little air or sanitation, but as one Cockney explained, 'We're living like bloody moles, but at least you can't 'ear Jerry'.

ABOVE AND LEFT: *In some stations, like the Elephant and Castle, the power was switched off at night and shelterers slung hammocks across the tracks. The branch line to Aldwych was closed and virtually given over to the shelterers who organized entertainments and were visited by an ENSA concert party and George Formby and his ukelele on the platform.*

RIGHT: *As thousands of city dwellers emerged from their homes after a raid to find the streets strewn with bricks and broken glass, and their homes a pile of rubble, 'the warden's day came and it was a glorious one': the ARP warden who had been regarded as a bit of a little Hitler himself when he'd been snooping around enforcing blackout regulations became 'the saviour of 'is country when the guns began to shoot'.*

BELOW: *A new word entered the language after the raid on Coventry on 14 November 1942. 'To coventrate' came to describe the concentrated bombing of any large town. Two hundred fires burned simultaneously, 550 people were killed and the cathedral was destroyed. The people of the beleaguered city, seen here fetching water after the raid, were to take the phoenix as their city's symbol of hope.*

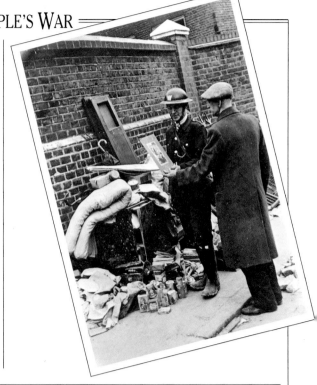

'It was as impersonal as a plague', wrote Evelyn Waugh, 'as though the city were infected with enormous venemous insects'. In the summer of 1944 London and the south-east faced another terror, the V1 flying bomb, or doodlebug or buzz bomb. The destruction of life and property was devastating.

ABOVE: *The aftermath of an attack.*

RIGHT: *Only one house in ten in inner London escaped the war unscathed.*

ABOVE: *The mobile canteen bought food and hot drinks to those people who had lost their cooking facilities – or their homes – and the canteens, which were run by a variety of voluntary agencies, were often a welcome sight and sustenance to the other emergency services at 'an incident'.*

RIGHT: *A Liverpool family bombed out of their home in Merseyside's 'May Week' in May 1941 when the area suffered eight successive nights of raids and the total of those killed was the highest outside London.*

LEFT: *'Keep the aspidistra flying'. The George Cross was instigated in 1940 for heroism on the home front. But when rescue workers in Bermondsey were asked to nominate some of their number for the honour, they replied 'Medals? We don't want no – medals. The whole – borough deserves a – medal'.*

LEFT: *By May 1941, one million four hundred thousand people – or one Londoner in every six – had been made homeless at some time or another. It was the East End that took the greatest battering. Officially the victims were encouraged to try to 'make their own arrangements where possible' – perhaps moving the entire family in with the similarly overcrowded next door neighbour?*

RIGHT: *Trying to get money for food, ration books, clothing, identity cards, replace essential furniture, find temporary accommodation, all could mean endless, frustrating traipsing between offices after the raids. A woman reported 'stranded in the Commercial Road crying with fatigue and despair' represented hundreds in need.*

BELOW: *When the raids of 1944 hit the capital, the social services had a more comprehensive and streamlined system of relief. A requisitioned dance hall in Lewisham served as an administrative centre with categories of distress dealt with under one roof.*

Business as Usual

'In a night the branch moved back to working conditions of a century earlier', wrote a City bank clerk after an air raid, 'all entries were made by hand in candlelight . . . letters were handwritten . . . no telephones were working'. The morning after a raid was a time for surveying the damage and seeing how to get to work. By the end of November 1940 the population of London had dropped by a quarter but absenteeism was rare. The slogan was 'London could take it' and its population set about proving that they could – and would.

TOP AND BOTTOM RIGHT: *It became a matter of pride for shops to carry on trading after a raid with defiant notices stuck up where the glass would have been; 'More Open than Usual'; 'We've had a close shave. Come in and get one yourself' outside a barber's; a pub's 'Our windows are gone but our spirits are excellent. Come in and try them'; and the all-purpose, succinct 'Blast'.*

BELOW: *Postmen struggled valiantly over rubble to deliver letters and the telegraph boys provided a mobile service.*

THE CHILDREN'S WAR

'**E**' Day came even before the declaration of war. On 1 September 1939, thousands of mothers with babies and small children,' and teachers in charge of school parties, assembled at railway stations in the cities for evacuation. Like soldiers, they didn't know where they were going, but they were labelled and despatched to the countryside where it was assumed they would be safe from whatever horrors war might bring.

The children were distributed by billeting officers, or claimed by householders as they arrived, tired, dirty and confused. Many of the evacuees came from the poorest and most overcrowded sections of the community and their hosts were frequently shocked by their waif-like, ill-clad, sometimes verminous condition – and often by their manners.

RIGHT: *Four thousand special trains were used to evacuate children from the cities with clockwork precision, but a child psychiatrist working in Cambridge regretted, 'if only the human effect had been worked out as carefully as the timetables'.*

The first to wave goodbye

Some children flourished in the countryside with kind families, fresh air, space and plentiful food. Some were desperately unhappy; a child from Liverpool sent her mother a card reading, 'Dear Mam, I want to come home. Pleas come and tack us home'.

By the beginning of 1940, four out of every ten children and nine-tenths of the mothers and children under five had gone home.

RIGHT: *There was a second wave of evacuation in the autumn of 1940 as the blitz intensified and a third in 1944 with the arrival of the 'flying bombs'.*

BELOW: *Mothers usually went with children under school age, but older children were on their own. Only one 'Visit an Evacuee' cheap day-return rail ticket was issued each month.*

LEFT: *The Government's Evacuation. Parents wave bravely as their children set off for evacuation with their school in north London in September 1939. The children grouped in the playground, singing songs like 'Ten Green Bottles' to keep their spirits up, and then marched off to the station, with parents left wondering if they would ever see their children again. 'Why are some mummies crying?' asked a small girl. 'Because they can't come on holiday with us too', her teacher replied.*

ABOVE: *The People's Evacuation. Women and children tramping through the fields out of Plymouth after nights of air raids. Homeless and exhausted families gathered up their possessions and trekked off for the open spaces, looking for peace and safety in the countryside.*

ABOVE: *The weather in September 1939 was glorious. Children evacuated to the countryside played in the sun, picked blackberries – and often pined terribly for home.*

ABOVE: *A world apart for children bombed out of their London homes was provided by Harold Nicolson and Vita Sackville-West, at Sissinghurst Castle in Kent.*

ABOVE: *'Grannie' Norris received the British Empire Medal in 1943 for her 'unremitting care' of a large number of children evacuated from London to her Kent home.*

Those Who Stayed

A householder could, if necessary, be compelled to billet evacuees; the decision to send children away was left to the parents – though pressure was considerable. 'Keep them happy, keep them safe', ran the government slogan. Although children may not have been safe in the cities, many parents still felt disturbed by their children's absence, whilst homesick children, for their part, were anxious for their parents. 'Rose cried herself to sleep every night for fear of what would happen to them if mother and father were killed in London', remembered one evacuee.

RIGHT: *A small girl sits drawing in the bombed-out shell of her parents' shop.*

LEFT: *Life went on, with lessons held in the shelters.*

BELOW: *A Stepney vicar has tea with a family of parishioners whose mother declared, in the face of his advice in November 1940, 'So far we're all right, we'll stay'.*

DON'T YOU KNOW THERE'S A WAR ON?

Churchill made some notes for a speech he was to make to the House of Commons in June 1940 at the height of the blitz: 'Learn to get used to it . . . Eels get used to skinning. Steady, continuous bombing, probably rising to greater intensity occasionally, must be regular condition of our lives. . .'

And so it became: the watchwords were, 'Don't you know there's a war on?' 'Make do and Mend', 'Lend don't Spend', 'in the war the term "battle-stained" is an honourable one'. Making the best of things became a talisman by which people carried on with dogged normality in the face of acute abnormality.

RIGHT: *People were encouraged to 'spend their holidays at home' and local councils laid on various entertainments, including orchestral concerts on a bomb site, dances in the park, Punch and Judy shows for the children, concert parties and parades, to make the idea attractive.*

'Kiss the boys goodbye'

'We'll meet again' went the song, but couples in wartime couldn't be sure that they would, so many got married, anxious to create what they hoped would be an island of certainty in those troubled times. A Camden Town jeweller sold thirty wedding rings in the first week of the war, compared to the usual three or four; and when call-up reached its peak in 1940, there were half a million weddings. Wedding dresses were borrowed or made from whatever material was available – butter muslin maybe, or parachute silk. Since icing sugar was unobtainable, wedding cakes were often iced cardboard confections borrowed from the baker and plopped over a wartime sponge cake. Honeymoons were brief or non existent – and all too often the bridegroom went straight back to war.

ABOVE: *A south-London bride gives a defiant wave as she leaves for her wedding from her bombed-out family home.*

ABOVE: *A deluge of confetti rains on the tin helmet of a bridegroom married in the sandbagged Islington Registry Office in 1940.*

LEFT: *'Business as Usual' on the pavement. Enthusiastic crowds clamour to buy up stock salvaged from a London shop hit during the previous night's raid.*

RIGHT: *Anderson shelters, which had to be dug into the ground and covered with three feet of soil, could give inspiration to keen gardeners yearning to create a rockery garden or daffodil hillock in their own back yard.*

BELOW: *'Eternal Father, Strong to Save'. During the war many clergymen noticed increases in their congregations and in the early months churches were often used as shelters – a sense of solid walls and a divine, protecting hand led people to pray 'lighten our darkness ... and protect us from the perils and dangers of this night' during the raids and blackout. Continuing to hold services in bombed-out churches became an act of faith and courage in itself. St Giles, Cripplegate, in 1941.*

ABOVE: *Usual activities in unusual places. This London office near Regent's Park was bombed out three times and the staff became accustomed to gathering their typewriters, files and whatever papers they could salvage, and getting on with the job in hand.*

LEFT: *Spirits were hard to come by, supplies of beer were erratic and often adulterated with oats and potatoes rather than barley, and diluted with water. Nevertheless the pub was still a popular place to go to meet friends – even if it was now a corrugated iron lean-to as was 'The Dolphin' in Coventry.*

RIGHT: *The elegant foyer of London's Savoy Hotel in the Strand was transformed into a first aid post to treat the victims of bomb damage.*

'We want not only the big man with the plough, but the little man with the spade to get busy this autumn', the Ministry of Agriculture exhorted. 'Let "Dig for Victory" be the motto ...' Lawns were turned into cabbage patches, runner beans usurped herbaceous borders and wasteland, bomb sites and railway embankments were dug up to 'grow more'.

LEFT: *The moat at the Tower of London provided allotments.*

RIGHT: *Chickens moved into towns and suburbs in an attempt to supplant the hated powdered egg. These hens were kept by ARP wardens at their post in Hackney. If you had less than twenty hens you were allowed to keep any eggs they laid – a considerable bonus when the ration was two eggs a week in 1941.*

BELOW: *Coal rationing and cold winters – there were 46° of frost in January 1942 – turned Britain into a nation of scavengers, collecting wood from bomb sites, woodlands and hedgerows and driftwood from the beaches, as here in Cornwall.*

'Make do and mend'

'When you feel tired of your old clothes, remember that by making them do you are contributing some part of an aeroplane, a gun or a tank', the President of the Board of Trade encouraged his audience. Clothes rationing started on Whit Sunday 1941 and women were urged to 'make do and mend' whilst a bossy 'Mrs Sew and Sew' recommended 'patriotic patches as something to be proud of'. The magazine *Housewife* encouraged there 'is a subtle bond between good looks and good morale. Put your best face forward'. So women lightened grey hair with Reckitt's blue, smeared beetroot juice on their lips and smoothed a mixture of shoe polish and face cream, or gravy browning, on their legs and drew a seam with an eyebrow pencil to simulate long-disappeared silk stockings.

ABOVE: *Hats were never rationed and became the fashion editor's standby as a frivolity for 'dressing-up' dowdy wartime clothes, and women were given tips for renovating a winter hat – often startlingly – for springtime, or turning an old felt hat into bedroom slippers.*

RIGHT: *Everything that could be was turned into something else: a coat from a candlewick bedspread, a blouse from dusters, a skirt from blackout material, a dress from a sheet or tablecloth, whilst surplus service blankets were seized upon and transformed into winter coats and dressing gowns.*

FIGHTING BACK

'We shall defend our island home . . . and outlive the menace of tyranny . . . we shall go on to the end. We shall defend our island whatever the cost may be. We shall fight on the beaches . . . we shall fight in the fields and streets, we shall fight in the hills, we shall never surrender . . .'

Winston Churchill speaking to the House of Commons the day after Dunkirk in May 1940 – and he is supposed to have added, under his breath, 'and beat the buggers about the head with bottles: that's all we've got.'

Now the fighting took place in the air and on the home front, preparing to repel the feared German invasion: 'Do not give the Germans anything. Do not tell him anything. Hide your maps. See that the enemy gets no petrol . . . Think always of your country before you think of yourselves'.

But it meant strengthening the attack as well as the defence. 'The war is driving Hitler back' – though it didn't seem much like it at the time when France had fallen, the Germans stood just across the Channel and the army's equipment had largely been left behind at Dunkirk. It was the first of Britain's darkest hours of the war. But Herbert Morrison, the new Minister of Supply, coined the slogan 'Go to it' – and the British people did.

RIGHT: *The 'V for Victory' campaign was promoted on the BBC and it got a tremendous response from the public. V-signs appeared everywhere, painted or chalked on walls, scratched on doors, embroidered on clothes, or, as here, made out of flowers. And, of course, the two-fingered V-sign was the trademark of Churchillian defiance.*

ABOVE: *Repelling the invader. Barbed wire was unrolled along the beaches of southern England and people were not allowed within ten miles of these flimsy defences without a permit.*

LEFT: *Sign posts and street names were removed to confuse the enemy, should he land – and they had the same effect on the natives. Travel became a nightmare of uncertainty as milestones, war memorials and anything else helpful were removed to be replaced with boards which vaguely pointed 'to the North' or 'to the West'.*

RIGHT: *Local Defence Volunteers (later to be known as the Home Guard) parked cars on the banks of the Great North Road ready to be swung across as a barricade should the German tanks (or a fifth column) be sighted.*

BELOW: *As a deterrent to planes or gliders landing airborne invasion troops, the flatlands of southern Britain – its commons, parks and fields – were littered with broken-down cars and lorries, buses, ploughs, barrels, iron bedsteads, rusty cooking ranges – a nation's scrap.*

The War on Waste

In 1940 the British people were asked to mobilize their detritus for the war effort:

'The war is driving Hitler back
But here's one way to win it.
Just give your salvage men the sack
And see there's plenty in it'.

The response was overwhelming: householders sorted their rubbish into separate bins, handed over saucepans they might never be able to replace and echoed the view heard during the salvage of iron railings ('we didn't shout when our sons were requisitioned, so why make a fuss about this?'). By the end of the war millions of tons of scrap and iron had been collected – much of which probably never left the scrapyard.

ABOVE: *Iron railings were removed from parks, churchyards, squares and private gardens to 'build battleships'. Many thought the unfenced squares more in keeping with a war effort designed to rally all.*

TOP RIGHT AND FAR RIGHT: *'Women of Britain give us your aluminium . . . we will turn your pots and pans into Spitfires and Hurricanes . . .' Hundreds and thousands of women obliged and felt 'a tiny thrill . . . as we hear news of an epic battle in the air . . . perhaps it is my saucepan that made part of the Hurricane'.*

BOTTOM RIGHT: *By August 1940 the rag-and-bone man was desribed by Herbert Morrison as 'the saviour of the nation' as his traditional cry of 'any old iron' took on a patriotic flavour.*

'Lend don't Spend', 'Lend to Attack', 'Fight in the streets – belong to your local savings group', 'Squash the Squander Bug': War Savings Weeks became a regular feature of wartime Britain with 'War Weapons' in 1940, 'Warships' in 1942, 'Wings for Victory' in 1943 and 'Save the Soldier' in 1944. The real importance of the savings was to keep inflation down, but the activities which the campaigns generated also served to keep up morale.

LEFT: Towns and cities competed with their neighbours in raising money for the war effort – money to be repaid after the war. Firms also competed setting targets: £20,000 for a Wellington Bomber, whilst smaller ones could aspire to £2,000 for an airplane wing.

BELOW: Pubs might aim to collect £138 for a 2,000lb bomb, or £30 for a sub-machine gun, whilst individuals could set their sights on raising the required 4 shillings for a hand grenade, or even 6d for a rivet.

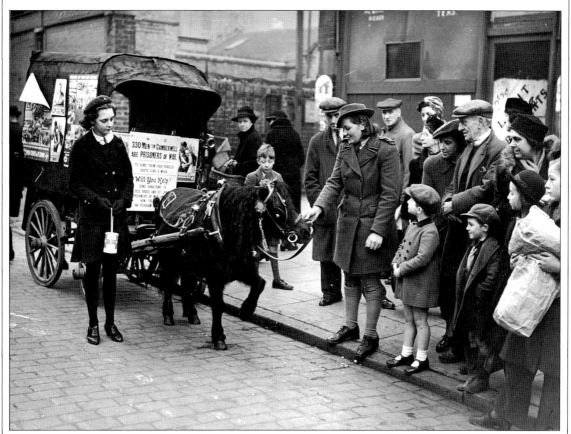

The Red Cross organized regular parcels to be sent to prisoners of war, to supplement those sent by their families, or to support POWs 'neglected' by their relatives. The parcels usually contained clothes, books and food.

ABOVE: *A Shetland pony and miniature covered wagon makes the rounds in Camberwell collecting to send parcels to 330 POWs from the borough.*

RIGHT: *'Doing the Lambeth Walk' for a Spitfire. A Spitfire was 'priced' at £5,000, and a town or borough could 'buy' a plane. The BBC gave a list of donations at the end of the nightly news. By April 1941, over £13 million had been raised by the hat being passed round in factories and pubs, or collecting boxes in shops and market stalls like this one organized by the market traders of Lambeth.*

Ammunition for the 'cold war'

'Knitting Socks for Soldiers' in 1940. A newspaper wittily suggested that with all that civilians were having to bear, it should be the soldiers knitting socks and comforters for the civilians instead.

The WVS, whose motto was 'If it should be done, the WVS will do it' mended, knitted and darned for troops and war workers – though one branch found that they were 'overwhelmed' with denim suits 'and the women do hate doing them'. One report in 1943 read 'our knitters do a good job . . . three of our battalions have asked for 2,500 socks, 1,500 pullovers and scarves and gloves in proportion to their other demands . . . and I always use up each month about 200 pairs of socks and 50 pullovers on my POWs'.

TOP RIGHT: *Reminiscent of early American quilting bees, Cornish women sit in the sun in August 1940 knitting socks for the troops – often using wool unravelled from old jumpers and pullovers.*

BOTTOM RIGHT: *All cinemas were closed by government order at the beginning of the war – but they were soon re-opened and, despite possible bomb damage in crowded places, cinema-going became one of the most popular forms of wartime entertainment. Usherettes at a Chester cinema 'do their bit' for the troops when the house lights go down.*

BELOW: *A 'knit-in' of comforters (or scarves) for the troops was a regular evening activity when homework was finished at this boy's prep school in Yorkshire in May 1940.*

LEFT: *'The fishermen are saving lives*
By sweeping seas for mines
So you'll not grumble, 'What no fish?'
When you have read these lines'.

Thus the Ministry of Food chided housewifes
as these fishermen assembled a Lewis gun
aboard their North Sea trawler.

ABOVE: *In 1943 the 'Bevin Boys' scheme –*
named after the Minister of Labour – was
introduced in a desperate attempt to raise the
production of coal. One in every ten men due
to be called up for the forces was chosen by
ballot to go down the mines instead. It was
not popular; it lacked any possible 'glamour'
associated with the forces and for the men –
who were usually about seventeen – it was a
salutary lesson in the hard work and
miserable pay of a life uderground.

WOMEN AT WAR

'She's the girl that makes the thing
that drills the hole that holds the spring
That drives the rod that turns the knob
that works the thingumebob.
. . . And it's the girl that makes the thing
that holds the oil that oils the ring
That works the thingumebob
THAT'S GOING TO WIN THE WAR.'

Popular song, 1942

B ritain's mobilization of women for the
'battle of production' went further than
any other country's except perhaps Rus-
sia. By 1943 it was almost impossible for a
woman under forty to avoid war work unless
she had very heavy family responsibilities, or
war workers billeted on her. Women went to
work in aircraft factories, engineering works,
chemical plants, munitions factories and filled
jobs vacated by men in public transport, as
postmen, railway workers, rent collectors,
house painters; they delivered milk and bread,
and joined the Women's Land Army. A booklet
issued to GIs arriving in Britain told them,
'women have proved themselves in this war'.

RIGHT: *Back to the land we must all lend a hand.*
There's a job to be done
Though we can't fire a gun
We can still do our bit with the hoe:
. . . We're all needed now,
We must all speed the plough
So come with us
Back to the land
The Women's Land Army was a hard and
underpaid way of winning the war: it paid
£1.85 (increased to £2.85 in 1944) for a
minimum 50-hour working week (much more
at harvest time): but 80,000 volunteered

ABOVE: *Women making barrage balloons worked twelve-hour shifts. By 1941 it was finally considered that they were 'strong enough' to handle the balloons they'd made. Soon half the barrage balloon sites in the country were operated by women.*

LEFT: *'They made the guns we need.' In the spirit of Louis MacNeice's* Swing-song:
> *'I'm only a wartime working girl,*
> *The machine shop makes me deaf.*
> *I have no prospects after the war*
> *And my young man is in the R.A.F.'*

RIGHT: *'Do you know that over 10,000 women are doing men's work on one British railway alone, acting as plate layers, and permanent way labourers, helping with maintenance work, clerks, ticket collectors, porters? Go to it! That's the way to do it! Put your back into it'.*

Essential work

Not all women could be in the 'front line' working in munitions factories or in the forces. They were doing work of a more traditional sort. At first, the government decreed that women stick to their jobs and their homes 'unless particularly well qualified'. But by 1943, 9 out of 10 single and 8 out of 10 married women were engaged in 'essential war work'.

RIGHT: *Women contributed to the war effort by undertaking part-time or voluntary work or chopping up wood salvaged from a bombing raid for firewood.*

BELOW: *'We're going to hang out the washing on the Siegfried Line' – 1,500 Army shirts a week at the Army Command in Aldershot.*

Rationing was first introduced in January 1940, and rationing was generally welcomed by housewives as a fairer system.

ABOVE: *Coal and coke were rationed, and had to be fetched from the depot.*

BELOW: *The first things to go 'on the ration' were butter, sugar, bacon and ham and more things were added every month. Bread was never rationed, nor was offal or fish. The housewife was encouraged to 'try a fish that's new'... whalemeat for example.*

BELOW: *The Home Front's contribution was vital too. 'I shop [and queue] with special care. I waste nothing … I try to keep myself and my house trim and cheerful. I take special pains with the cooking because I know this keeps the men's spirits up. Though I may not win medals, I am certainly helping to win the war.'*

HAVING FUN

'When you're up to your neck in hot water
Be like the kettle and sing'.

G lenn Miller played 'Little Brown Jug' and
'Moonlight Serenade': at various stages
of the war, troops and civilians joined in
'MacNamara's Band', 'Moonlight Becomes
You', 'Wish Me Good Luck As You Wave Me
Goodbye', 'Is You Is Or Is You Not My Baby?'.
They changed the words of 'You Are My Sun-
shine' to 'You Are My Woodbine' – clearly an
equal compliment in days of acute cigarette
shortages; and, rather surprisingly, the German
song 'Lili Marlene' became one of the great wartime hits to equal the First World War's 'Tipper-
ary'. The Ministry of Information was unable to
commission a rival that caught on.

People listened to the wireless with Tommy
Handley and Richard Murdoch in *ITMA* (It's
That Man Again) or *The Brains Trust* with Pro-
fessor Joad and Sir Julian Huxley as regulars.

Or they went to the cinema. Between 25 and
30 million cinema tickets were sold every week,
and audiences crammed in to watch films
about the war, like *The Way Ahead* or *In Which
We Serve* (with a script by Noel Coward), or
films about other wars, with Laurence Olivier in
Henry V or Clark Gable in *Gone With The Wind*.

RIGHT: *There were also the wartime dances,
held anywhere there was room to foxtrot or do
the Palais Glide or the Lambeth Walk, to
boogie woogie or to jitterbug: in church halls,
factories, fire stations, village halls, Nissen
huts, US airforce bases, Red Cross Clubs –
even, at a pinch, your own front room.*

BELOW: *Disappointment at the seaside. In the beautiful summer of 1940, English beaches were festooned with barbed wire to 'repel the invader', piers were blown up or mined, and concrete gun enplacements dug into the cliffs. It seemed an inadequate deterrent against a serious force, and the poet, Laurie Lee, expressed the mood in* Seafront:

'Here the maze of our bewilderment
The thorn-crowned wire spreads
*   high along the shore*
And flowers with rust
*   and tears our commmon sun.'*

ABOVE: *Blackpool, where 'fun' could still be had if you could get the transport, find a hotel and remember to take your own sheets, towel, soap and ration book. Resorts were not supposed to encourage visitors in wartime.*

ABOVE: *Ivy Benson and her All Girl Band entertain US troops, whose wartime favourites included the poignant 'Don't Sit Under the Apple Tree' (with anyone else but me).*

ABOVE: *The 'Old Masters' moved out of the National Gallery and 1s lunchtime concerts for war workers moved in. The piano recitals of Myra Hess (seen playing at the Royal Exchange in 1942) attracted long queues. The audience sat on the floor eating their sandwiches, and the WVS 'supplied a good cup of coffee with synthetic cream for 6d'.*

ABOVE: *'We'll Meet Again', 'The White Cliffs of Dover', 'Yours': Vera Lynn was the forces' sweetheart. Her radio programme* Sincerely Yours *was 'a sentimental half hour linking the men in the forces with their womenfolk at home – though fears were expressed in high places that this concession to feelings might 'sap the fighting man's morale'.*

'Workers' Playtime.'

You couldn't 'Go to it' all the time. But a BBC
handbook of 1942 made a little leisure after a
12-hour shift seem all part of the war effort:
'Rest from work has become a precious thing –
and, because the quality of work depends so
largely upon it, one of great value.'

ABOVE: *ENSA was set up in 1940 to tour the
country, entertaining the troops and war
workers. Sometimes the music, concert parties
and comedians did great things for morale –
but not always: on one occasion, a man
jumped on stage after a performance calling
for 'three cheers for the audience'.*

ABOVE: *'Roll Out the Barrel'. Fire guards around the piano in their canteen in Southampton. Another popular piano singsong was 'Knees Up Mother Brown'.*

ABOVE: *Dancing at Rainbow Corner, Piccadilly, the club run by the American Red Cross for the GIs, where they could drink coke, play crap, shoot pool – and jitterbug.*

RIGHT: *'The civil and economic destruction in Plymouth exceeds anything we've seen elsewhere', wrote a Mass Observer after the terrible raids of Spring 1941. But the city 'made an impressive show of courage and cheerfulness . . . strong local pride and a tradition of toughness associated with the sea, make people determined to show that they can take it' . . . as they danced on the promenade.*

LEFT: *In 1940 thousands of French troops arrived in Britain. Like the Free French leader, General de Gaulle, they felt that with the fall of France, they had lost the battle but not the war. Whilst awaiting their chance of victory, they kept their independence by celebrating 14 July on foreign soil, but with Gallic elegance and gaiety.*

LEFT: *'The stolen crowded moments fly
Too fragile in this breathing space.'*

*A wife visits her soldier husband at his
barracks as the troops prepare to go overseas.*

ABOVE: *'Oh my darling, O my pet
Whatever else you may forget
In yonder isle beyond the sea
Do not forget you've married me.'*

...r Victory

'...is is your victory', Churchill told the crowds thronging Whitehall on 8 May 1945. It was peace at last – at least in Europe.

But now Hitler was dead in his bunker in Berlin and bunting was off ration – at least until the end of May. All over Britain the sky was lit up with a rosy glow – but this time it wasn't the blitz, it was bonfires lit in parks, gardens, on commons, everywhere. There were street parties, crowds danced the hokey cokey in the middle of the road, and when someone let off a firework in Piccadilly, a wit called out, 'Don't worry, it's one of ours'.

TOP RIGHT: *Civilians and soldiers celebrate.*

BOTTOM RIGHT: *The Royal Family, who had shared Britain's war with the people, with Winston Churchill – the man who had led them to victory but who would be voted out of office now that peace had come.*

RIGHT: *Ecstatic crowds dance in Piccadilly.*

BELOW: *The end of the day: bonfire celebrations in Croydon.*